LONDON PUBLIC LIBRARY
WITHDRAWN

We'll Never Forget

by Jean Miso

Remembrance is the heart of Canadian pride
Jean Miso

Text copyright © 2010 Jean Miso

Lyrics copyright © 2009 Jean Miso

Illustration copyright © 2010 Asher Sadeh and Jean Miso. Illustrations the property of Jean Miso.

All rights reserved. No part of this book may be reproduced in any manner without the express written consent of Jean Miso.

Jean Miso, 11 Sagamore Crescent, Toronto, Ontario, M9C 4G3

www.jeanmiso.ca

Library and Archives Canada Cataloguing in Publication

Miso, Jean, 1961-

We'll never forget / written by Jean Miso ; illustrated by Asher Sadeh.

Based on an original song of the same title.
Includes a CD with a choral version and an accompaniment track.

ISBN 978-0-9866938-0-9

1. Remembrance Day (Canada)—Juvenile literature.

I. Sadeh, Asher II. Title.

D680.C2M57 2010   j394.264   C2010-905138-6

Coin image © 2010 Royal Canadian Mint – All Rights Reserved

The Poppy, when used as a symbol of Remembrance in Canada, is a trademark of the Dominion Command of The Royal Canadian Legion and is used with their kind permission.

Acknowledgements

Support for the creation of this book came in many forms. One form of support is valued no more or less than another.

Laura Brooks first encouraged me to publish my song, and for this encouragement I owe her a great debt of thanks.

I thank the financial supporters of this book: the Friends of 48th Highlanders of Canada Museum, Sports NRG and the ETCU Financial Credit Union Limited. Their generous contributions reduced the costs of publishing.

I send heartfelt thanks to the staff of Sunnybrook Health Sciences Centre in Toronto: Virginia McLaughlin, Doris Guyatt, Dorothy Ferguson, Nancy Bowers-Ivanski, Julie Pepin and Jacqueline Chelsky. They helped make my interviewing of veterans in K and L Wings smooth and pleasurable, and embraced this book by hosting the book launch.

I gratefully acknowledge the support provided by the following military officers: Honorary Lieutenant-Colonel John Newman; Major (Ret.) George Pearce, CD; Major W.P. "Bud" Gillie, MMM, CD; and Brigadier-General (Ret.) Greg Young, OMM, CD. They graciously answered countless questions and provided me with special access to military functions.

A special thank you goes to Anne Broughton, Cate Goodwin, Quinn Hache, Jordan Davis and Tess Lavelle-Sutton. They donated their talents and time in preparing the vocal track of the music CD. A sincere thank you also goes to guitarist Ty Price whose passionate accompaniment embraces the spirit in which the song was composed.

I sincerely appreciate the contributions of Robert DiVito at Montgomery Sound and Image Studio, my illustrator Asher Sadeh, my friend and editor Franklin Carter, proofreader Elizabeth Cockle, Web site designer Lathieeshe Thillainathan, and graphics and layout designer Dr. Grafix. All paid close attention to detail and gave their very best work.

Lastly, the support from my loving family Dan, Emerson and Austin, my parents Paul and Clara McKenzie, and my brothers Dave, Art and Don and their families makes me feel like the luckiest person alive. This book is evidence of our McKenzie family motto: "No goal is too high if you aim with care and confidence."

Preface

This book is dedicated with gratitude to all Canadian Forces men and women, both past and present, who have voluntarily given of themselves to serve our country with pride and fortitude. The song "We'll Never Forget" was inspired by the memory of my grandfather Elmer Moses (E.M.) McKenzie who was a World War I veteran.

By interviewing the military men and women who are featured in this book—and by speaking with many other military people as well—I have learned that at the core of every soldier is a sense of duty. Soldiers put society's needs ahead of their own to protect Canada's freedom and way of life. Since World War I, more than 100,000 Canadian soldiers have died before their natural time defending their steadfast beliefs. Many who were fortunate to have survived war and peacekeeping duties have suffered permanent injuries.

Our Canadian military heroes bear the darkness of war within them. They have borne witness to horrendous events that affect the very fibre of their being. By reading my grandfather's war diary and by interviewing the military contributors to this book, I realize that their life-changing experiences created an unwavering bond among them. Like a close-knit family, they dearly embrace traditions, and the elder members groom the youth to carry on our proud Canadian military history.

With all my heart, I thank each of the military men and women who have generously shared their personal stories and perspectives on war. Their messages and examples emphasize the importance of Canadian citizenship, responsibility, teamwork, cooperation, integrity and respect. Their portraits in this book promote positive character attributes that teachers can infuse into their curricula throughout the school year. Reading the words of our Canadian heroes inspires us all to work for peace every day of the year.

Acting Sergeant Elmer Moses (E.M.) McKenzie, MM
Honours and Awards:
Military Medal
Army, World War I (1914–18)

Elmer McKenzie was 17 years old when he joined the Canadian army in 1915. He voluntarily enlisted to keep his older brother Doug company while overseas.

At the beginning of his duty, Private McKenzie was a runner. He then trained as a scout and later became an intelligence observer. These jobs required him to go at night into no man's land (an area between the two opposing armies' lines), collect information that would help Canadian troops and then report back to his commander.

Elmer McKenzie fought in three major battles in France and Belgium: the Battle of the Somme, the Battle of Vimy Ridge and the Battle of Passchendaele. These and other battles were significant because Canadian soldiers proved that they were an impressive force and earned the respect of Allied troops.

E.M.'s war diary shows that he was guided by unshakeable values such as the safeguarding of friendships and love of country. He believed it was important to stay connected with family and friends in Canada and Ireland by exchanging letters and packages.

He was also willing to take up different challenges to improve as a Canadian soldier. Near the end of the war, E.M. McKenzie was promoted to Acting Sergeant. He applied for a place in the Royal Air Force, and was accepted.

Acting Sergeant McKenzie would want you to follow his example by getting a good education to prepare yourself for all of life's challenges.

Petty Officer Don Cameron—pictured here at age 19—spent six years between September 3, 1939 and August 31, 1945 on board various escort destroyers. He served as a Leading Signalman in the Royal Canadian Navy. His first ship was the HMCS Ottawa.

The destroyers helped protect convoys of Canadian commercial ships as they travelled eastward from Halifax across the Atlantic Ocean. The ships carried food, ammunition, fuel and Canadian soldiers to help Allied troops in Britain. In a convoy, all crews had to work together to protect one another from surface raiders and enemy submarines.

A convoy typically consisted of five lanes of ships with 10 ships in each lane. The convoy moved at eight knots per hour or at the pace of the slowest vessel. The ships usually took three weeks to travel across the ocean to reach a British port.

"Teamwork builds success," Petty Officer Cameron says.

Petty Officer Don Cameron, CD
Honours and Awards:
Canadian Forces Decoration
Navy, World War II (1939–45)

Mervin Fisher grew up on a farm. When he was 16 years old, he decided to join the militia to make money to support his mother. He enlisted a year later at age 17 in the Canadian army. He consistently sent half of his pay to his mother every month.

Private Fisher was trained to work with an armoured corps; however, he served as an infantryman in Belgium and later in Holland. During his tour, he was captured and held in a prisoner-of-war camp called Stalag 11B. Fortunately, he was treated well by his captors. Yet for much of his adult life, Mervin felt guilty about being captured and thought that he had not served his country to the best of his ability.

Private Fisher would like you to learn from his experience.

"Do the best that you can do in this world," he says. "Things will work out."

Private Mervin Fisher
Army, World War II

Freedom is a gift
that Canadian soldiers gave.

Chief Warrant Officer Kevin R. Junor, MMM, CD
Honours and Awards:
Member of the Order of Military Merit;
Canadian Forces Decoration
Canadian Forces (Army), Sierra Leone

Chief Warrant Officer Kevin Junor is a proud 30-year member of the Toronto Scottish Regiment. During his military career, he was a Regimental Sergeant Major and a military adviser. He wanted to help rebuild countries that had been torn apart by conflict. Kevin eventually travelled to Sierra Leone in West Africa.

In Sierra Leone, Chief Warrant Officer Junor served with the International Military Advisory and Training Team from June to December 2007. The team, which had 105 military people (including 11 Canadian soldiers) from several nations, trained and advised Sierra Leone's soldiers. Kevin worked closely with three battalions of troops (or roughly 1,200 soldiers) in the northern part of the country.

Chief Warrant Officer Junor found out quickly that this poor country could barely support its military. Although Sierra Leone's soldiers were paid with money, each soldier was also partly paid with three cups of rice each day. Kevin Junor recalls that the soldiers of Sierra Leone sometimes did not receive their rations, yet they were expected to perform their duties while hungry. They had barely enough to survive.

To effect positive changes in Sierra Leone's military, Kevin knew that he would have to educate himself about the local culture and respect the people. Before his tour had ended, Chief Warrant Officer Junor felt that he was among family.

"They taught me what it was like to be a black man in Africa and I got in touch with my ancestry," he says. "The people of Sierra Leone were warm and welcoming, and they gave continuously from what little they had. They did their very best and had personal pride."

Before he departed from Sierra Leone, Kevin Junor received an honour from his African colleagues. He was named "Konkor Marah" after the legendary African Regimental Sergeant Major.

We are safe in Canada because they all were brave.

Captain Lloyd G. Queen, MC
Honours and Awards:
Military Cross
Army, World War II

Captain Lloyd Queen belonged to the proud Fort Garry Horse Regiment of Winnipeg. Up to World War I, the regiment rode on horseback, but by World War II the horses had been replaced by Sherman tanks.

In 1943, Lloyd Queen was sent overseas to serve Canada. He was second in command of a squadron that consisted of 30 tanks. Each tank had a crew of five whose lives depended on each team member carrying out his duties and trusting in Captain Queen's command. Lloyd needed to have complete confidence in each soldier and expected them to perform their duties with precision. In battle, Lloyd Queen took the initiative, always maintaining close radio contact with his squadron and his commander.

Within his six years of service, Captain Queen became Aide-de-Camp (a distinguished title) to Canada's Major-General Daniel Spry. Lloyd also received the Military Cross for bravery from King George VI.

Today, Lloyd Queen speaks publicly at five to 10 schools each year about Remembrance Day. Like other veterans, he realizes that if he remains silent, young Canadians like you will not understand the horrors of war and the sacrifices made throughout Canadian history.

"All war is really very horrid, and it should be the last thing we do to resolve conflict," he says.

Poppies remember those at war who died.

Lieutenant-Colonel J.G. Philippe Bérard, CD
Honours and Awards:
Canadian Forces Decoration
Canadian Forces (Army), Chief of Staff

At the age of 13, Philippe Bérard dreamed of becoming a teacher. But when he joined the Army Cadets, he soon realized that he could apply teaching skills within this organization. By age 17, he had earned the rank of Sergeant Major and was leading 400 cadets in learning survival skills at a summer camp program.

When he joined the Canadian Forces at age 18, Philippe Bérard considered himself fortunate because he was selected for a specialized program called the Officer Candidate Training Program. Typically, candidates were required to have more than a high school education; however, Philippe's potential was recognized and the requirement was waived with the understanding that he would finish a university degree, which he completed nine years later.

For the next 25 years, Lieutenant-Colonel Bérard held many responsible positions within the Canadian military. He started as a Second Lieutenant in a platoon of the Royal 22nd Regiment, which is more commonly known as the Van Doos. Philippe served our country with pride in peacetime Cyprus and West Germany. In 2006, he achieved the highest level of bilingual status when he was declared proficient in both English and French, Canada's official languages.

Today Lieutenant-Colonel Bérard is the Chief of Staff of 32 Canadian Brigade Group. He says the job is like being the master of an orchestra. He leads and directs the work of the staff at headquarters.

"Believe in what you are doing," Philippe Bérard advises. "What you are doing today is the basis of what you will become later on."

At the age of 87, Beth Hancock says that she never regretted following her instincts and enlisting in the Women's Royal Canadian Naval Service (the WRENs) at the age of 19. As a young woman, Beth received six months of basic training in Galt, Ontario. Her pay for enlisted service was 90 cents per day. After her training was complete, Beth was posted at naval headquarters in Ottawa. She and other team members in this "confidential" department received secret information that they passed on through the chain of command. Maintaining secrecy in wartime was necessary.

WREN Writer Robinson was then ordered to Scotland for a two-year deployment. She worked at the Canadian base HMCS Niobe. She made sure that navy staff received payment for their work. Beth feels that her military career provided her with a hands-on education. Away from base, Beth lived on the grounds of a nearby country estate called Langhouse. She was quartered with seven other women in a Nissen hut that overlooked the village of Inverkip. Although the living conditions were modest, WREN Writer Robinson believes her wartime experience enriched her character.

"I learned respect because we had to live with so many other people," she says. "At the same time, we had to learn to take commands from the officers."

Today, Beth Hancock offers this advice to young people: "Listen to your inner voice and let it be your guide."

WREN Writer Beth Robinson (Married Name: Hancock)
Navy, World War II

Guy Lavergne grew up as the second youngest of 12 children in Témiscaming, Quebec. He had a bilingual education, learning his subjects in the morning in French and then learning his subjects in the afternoon in English. Guy's love of languages attracted him to the army because he wanted to learn Korean and Japanese.

In 1950, the Korean War broke out and Guy Lavergne joined the army. He was assigned to the 2nd Battalion of the Princess Patricia's Canadian Light Infantry. He fought in the war and remained in the army for 28 years, providing dedicated military service to Canada.

A man with an adventurous spirit, Master Corporal Guy Lavergne advises you to reach beyond the familiar to fulfill your dreams.

Master Corporal Guy Lavergne
Army, Korean War (1950–53)

Men and women gave their all,

Norman Direnfeld was five years old when he immigrated to Canada from Poland. His family settled in the small town of Wynyard, Saskatchewan, near the Quill Lakes. When he was 19 years old, before the draft came into effect in 1944, Norman volunteered to join the Canadian navy.

In World War II, Petty Officer Direnfeld served on a ship called the HMCS Stettler, a frigate that was named after a town in Alberta. As a Radio Artificer, 4th Class, he operated and repaired the ship's radar. His job involved keeping the radar operational so that his crewmen could detect the enemy at and above the water line. Other crew members maintained sonar equipment that searched for submarines. The crew sometimes used improvised spare parts to make repairs.

After the war, Armed Forces personnel could enroll in any Canadian university without cost. Norman received $60 per month to cover his expenses. He was ecstatic to have the opportunity to attend the University of Manitoba and to earn an engineering degree from McGill University in Montreal. "The best thing in the world was getting a free education," he says.

Norman encourages you to get a solid education because he recognizes that in life you can lose everything material, but you can never lose your knowledge.

Petty Officer Norman Direnfeld
Navy, World War II

In 1943, at the age of 20, Mona Morrow enlisted in the armed services. She intended to serve Canada as a hospital assistant, but she became an Airwoman in the Royal Canadian Air Force (RCAF) instead.

During her training, Mona was asked to join a group of entertainers called the RCAF Blackouts. This group consisted of 10 Airwomen and 20 Airmen. The RCAF Blackouts toured England and newly liberated countries such as France, Belgium, Holland and Germany.

The group went to the front lines and often presented two variety shows each day. Each show was 1.5 hours in length and more than 200 people watched each show. Mona and the other cast members of the Blackouts tried to make each show special for members of all branches of the military.

Mona's role during World War II was essential to Canada's war effort because she lifted the spirits and morale of our troops so that they could perform their duties to the best of their abilities.

Today, Mona Shaw says that her role in World War II taught her that a positive attitude will boost the morale of others.

Airwoman 2 Mona Morrow (Married Name: Shaw)
Air Force, World War II

standing side by side.

Major Thomas A. Nguyen, CD
Honours and Awards:
Canadian Forces Decoration
Canadian Forces (Army), Peacekeeping

Thomas Nguyen was born in Saigon, Vietnam. When he was seven years old, his family escaped from Vietnam and came to Canada for a better life. Later, Thomas joined the army to express his gratitude to Canada for taking in his family and providing them with a safe place to live.

In his 17 years of military service, Major Nguyen has travelled overseas three times to perform peacekeeping duties in Bosnia, Haiti and Sudan. He has performed different roles and demonstrated great flexibility in each country. In Bosnia, he was a Detachment Commander who carried out National Command's directions. In Haiti, Major Nguyen served as an assistant to the Chief of Staff. In Sudan, he was a military observer.

While overseas, Major Nguyen saw many people struggling daily for survival, and he knew that people in Canada lived comparatively luxurious lives. He observed that people in wartorn countries often need much less—such as a bowl of rice—than many Canadians need to make them happy.

"Giving to your country and to the world is a path filled with pride," Major Nguyen says. "There are many roads that lead to positive contributions for others. Choose one!"

Ron Alkema joined the army at age 17 and has proudly served our country for more than 30 years. He has been deployed four times during his career. He performed duties as a peacekeeper in Cyprus in 1985 and 1992. Ron served as a military adviser in Sierra Leone in 2006. He spent six months in Afghanistan in 2008–09.

As part of a peacekeeping team, Captain Alkema helped create a buffer zone between warring groups and never shows favouritism to either side. He has seen countries fractured by civil strife and has channelled his military career into helping those countries stabilize so that they may rebuild and repair.

"My hope is for people to live in safe and secure surroundings like we have in Canada," Captain Alkema says. "We have a great country that we can be proud of and celebrate."

Captain Ron Alkema, CD
Honours and Awards:
Canadian Forces Decoration
Canadian Forces (Army), Peacekeeping

Poppies remember those at war who died.

Shangary Satgunanathan was born in Sri Lanka and moved to Canada when she was 15 years old. She became a Canadian citizen at the age of 18. Shangary never took for granted the freedom and opportunity that our country offers, and she hopes that people living in Canada do not take the privileges that this country offers for granted either. "I am so grateful for my life in Canada," she says.

While still a student in 2001, Shangary Satgunanathan joined the Canadian army as a medic. Eight years later, she deployed to Afghanistan. She worked 12-hour shifts in the patient administration division of a NATO hospital at Kandahar's airfield. Part of Corporal Shangary Satgunanathan's job was ensuring that patients and visitors were cleared of unsafe items before they entered the hospital.

Corporal Satgunanathan is a proud Canadian soldier. She believes that serving in the Canadian Forces is an honour and would gladly sign up for another six-month tour.

Corporal Shangary Satgunanathan
Canadian Forces (Army), Afghanistan (2001–)

John Gibson grew up near Halifax, Nova Scotia, in a Mi'kmaq family with 16 brothers and sisters. At age 12, he left home to earn $1.25 each day working on an apple farm in the Annapolis Valley.

When John was 14 years old, he joined the reserves of the West Nova Scotia Regiment. Three years later, he transferred to the Royal Canadian Regiment. His last change of regiment took him to Ipperwash near London, Ontario. He was part of the 2nd Battalion of the Queen's Own Rifles.

Sergeant Gibson served eight years in the army and performed two tours of duty in Korea. He remembers how difficult it was for him on his first tour of duty: he served 418 days on the front line before he got a seven-day leave to Tokyo. "I felt proud of my citizenship and of serving Canada," he says.

After his army days, John Gibson settled happily into civilian life. He spent 16 years as a horse driver for a paper mill in Halifax. He later became a baker and still loves to make apple pies and cakes.

Living in Canada is a privilege, he believes, because Canada gives him the freedom to choose the life he wishes to lead.

Sergeant John Gibson
Army, Korean War

In the world around us, Canadians do their part.

Semi-military discipline and order were very much a part of Bud Gillie's life as a youth. He was a member of the Boys' Brigade, a group that promoted youth excellence and leadership. His later entry into the Canadian Armed Forces seemed a natural way to further his goal of serving Canada.

In 1985–86, Major Gillie saw active duty as a peacekeeper in Cyprus. He was responsible for arranging the logistics of army transportation. Since 2009, he has served as the Commanding Officer of a medical unit called the 25 (Toronto) Field Ambulance. This unit responds to the initial medical needs of injured or ill soldiers; it acts much like a paramedic unit does in civilian life.

"Whether you are a soldier or a civilian, you need to be prepared," Major Gillie says. He not only states these words, he also lives by them.

After 33 years of service, Major Gillie continues to pursue a military career. When he is not soldiering, he is a leader in the Scouts Canada.

Major William P. "Bud" Gillie, MMM, CD
Honours and Awards:
Member of the Order of Military Merit;
Canadian Forces Decoration
Canadian Forces (Army), Peacekeeping

Dave Crook was 18 years old when he joined the 2nd Battalion of the Princess Patricia's Canadian Light Infantry. As a private in the Korean War, he helped maintain a position for three days while being surrounded and cut off from Allied support. For his bravery and steadfast behaviour in battle, he received a presidential citation from the government of the United States.

Today, Dave Crook remembers the wartime hardships of living outside through two harsh winters and being dug into a hole in the ground with only one blanket to keep him warm. He says, "I did it for this beautiful country."

The army helped Sergeant Major Crook learn about life and helped him place value on what is important. "Material things are not important to me," he says. "Remembering you are Canadian is."

A man of excellent character, Sergeant Major Dave Crook proudly and faithfully served Canadians for 29 years in the military.

Sergeant Major Dave Crook, CD
Honours and Awards:
Canadian Forces Decoration and Clasp;
U.S. Presidential Citation; Syngman Rhee War Medal
Army, Korean War

Warrant Officer Paul Baytor
Air Force, World War II

At 88 years of age, Paul Baytor readily remembers the badge number—R194189—that was assigned to him in World War II when he enlisted in the Royal Canadian Air Force. He was 20 when he signed up. Just two years earlier, he had become a proud Canadian citizen. He had moved to Canada from Czechoslovakia.

During the war, Paul Baytor earned the rank of Warrant Officer and served as a trained wireless air gunner (WAG). To become a WAG, Warrant Officer Baytor had to become proficient with Morse code, signals, mathematics and the procedures of the RCAF. In fact, Paul became a wireless instructor at L'Ancienne-Lorette, Quebec, before setting out to Scotland and then England.

In Europe, Warrant Officer Baytor flew primarily at night in aircraft such as Wellingtons and Halifaxes. He was one of seven crew members on a plane. Warrant Officer Baytor operated the radar and translated the incoming Morse code messages from Bomber Command for the crew. He was able to decode approximately 10–12 words per minute.

Paul Baytor cherishes the three years that he was enlisted in the RCAF. The memories are among the most interesting and happiest in his life. He wants everyone in Canada to know this message: "Communication is important!"

Translated into Morse code, Paul's message looks like this:

−·−· −−− −− −− ··− −· ·· −·−· ·− − ·· −−− −· / ·· ··· / ·· −− ·−·· −−− ·−· − ·− −· −

(Each letter is separated by a space, and each word is separated by a slash.)

Company Quarter Master Sergeant Herb Pike
Army, World War II

At 15 years of age and with only a Grade 10 education, Herb Pike was the breadwinner in his family. He worked 12 hours each day with a pick and shovel. He earned very little money. Three years later, he enlisted in the army to receive a steady income from the government of Canada to support his mother.

Four-and-a-half years of service as a soldier during World War II forged Company Quarter Master Sergeant Pike's character, ethics and love of Canada. He especially values discipline and the willingness to work hard. He recommends these virtues to all Canadians.

"My school was the army and the people I met were my teachers," he says.

Herb Pike's fellow soldiers are as close to him as brothers. "If you have people looking after your back," he says, "they are extra special."

Company Quarter Master Sergeant Pike was thrilled to be selected as one of several veterans to appear in a television commercial which featured a 2005 "Year of the Veteran" 25-cent circulation coin produced by the Royal Canadian Mint. Both the commercial and the coin honoured all veterans for their contributions to Canada and the sacrifices that they made on our behalf.

Brigadier-General Greg Young, OMM, CD
Honours and Awards:
Order of Military Merit;
Canadian Forces Decoration 3;
Legion of Merit;
Afghan Medal of Bravery

Canadian Forces (Army), Afghanistan

Brigadier-General Greg Young has dedicated more than four decades of outstanding service to Canada. Rising from the rank of Private soldier, he is highly regarded by his military colleagues for his compassion, determination and hands-on approach to leadership.

As the Deputy Commanding General of the United States Combined Security Transition Command—Afghanistan with responsibility for the reforming of the Afghan National Police, Brigadier-General Young worked to improve security in Afghanistan. He also acted as a mentor to that country's Deputy Minister for Security. His efforts were recognized by the government of Afghanistan, which awarded him the State's Medal for Bravery, and the government of the United States, which awarded him the Legion of Merit medal.

When signing off any correspondence, Brigadier-General Young uses the phrase "Strength and Honour." He believes that strength of character and performing one's duty honourably reflect not only your personal values but also those of your organization and your nation.

"Afghanistan was and is an honourable mission," he says. "Canadians are there trying to help provide the security that country needs to recover and rebuild itself. Everyone faces obstacles and it is necessary to use your strength of character to conduct yourself honourably as you confront those obstacles. That is true in Afghanistan and it is true in life."

Canadian troops
are heroes,
we're forever in their debt.

Colonel Robert Dale, DSO, DFC, CD

Honours and Awards:
Distinguished Service Order;
Distinguished Flying Cross;
Canadian Forces Decoration

Air Force, World War II

Robert Dale was one of many high school graduates who felt compelled to sign up for military duty in World War II. His sense of responsibility stemmed from Canadian pride and a family tradition he wished to continue. His father was a medical officer in World War I, and his brother Geoffrey served overseas in World War II with the Toronto Scottish Regiment.

Robert Dale's interest in aircraft led him into the Royal Canadian Air Force. During the war, he served overseas in Bomber Command of the RAF as a Navigator on Wellington and Mosquito aircraft. When plotting a course for his plane, Colonel Dale considered factors such as wind speed (because wind could easily send his aircraft off course if the speed wasn't calculated properly) and even the location of the moon and stars. He plotted many successful night flights that typically lasted seven or more hours.

In June 1944, following an air reconnaissance in a Mosquito, Colonel Dale made what was perhaps his most important contribution to World War II. His analysis of the weather conditions over Europe and the Atlantic prompted a 24-hour postponement of the D-Day invasion so that the Allies could take advantage of better weather. For his service in World War II, Colonel Dale earned the Distinguished Service Order, the Distinguished Flying Cross and the Canadian Forces Decoration.

After the war, Robert Dale completed his education and worked successfully as a businessman. He also served on the Board of Directors of Sunnybrook Health Sciences Centre in Toronto and as Chairman of its Veterans Advisory Committee.

Colonel Dale was also involved with the Air Cadet League of Canada, helping to develop good citizenship, leadership and physical fitness in young people aged 12–18 years. After 65 years of service with the Air Cadets, Robert Dale earned the title of Honorary President of the League.

"The most important thing people can possess is pride in their country," he says to all Canadians. "That is why I went to war: to preserve our freedom. If we had lost the war, things would have been terribly different."

Poppies remember those at war who died.

We'll Never Forget

Words and Music by Jean Miso
© 2009 All rights reserved

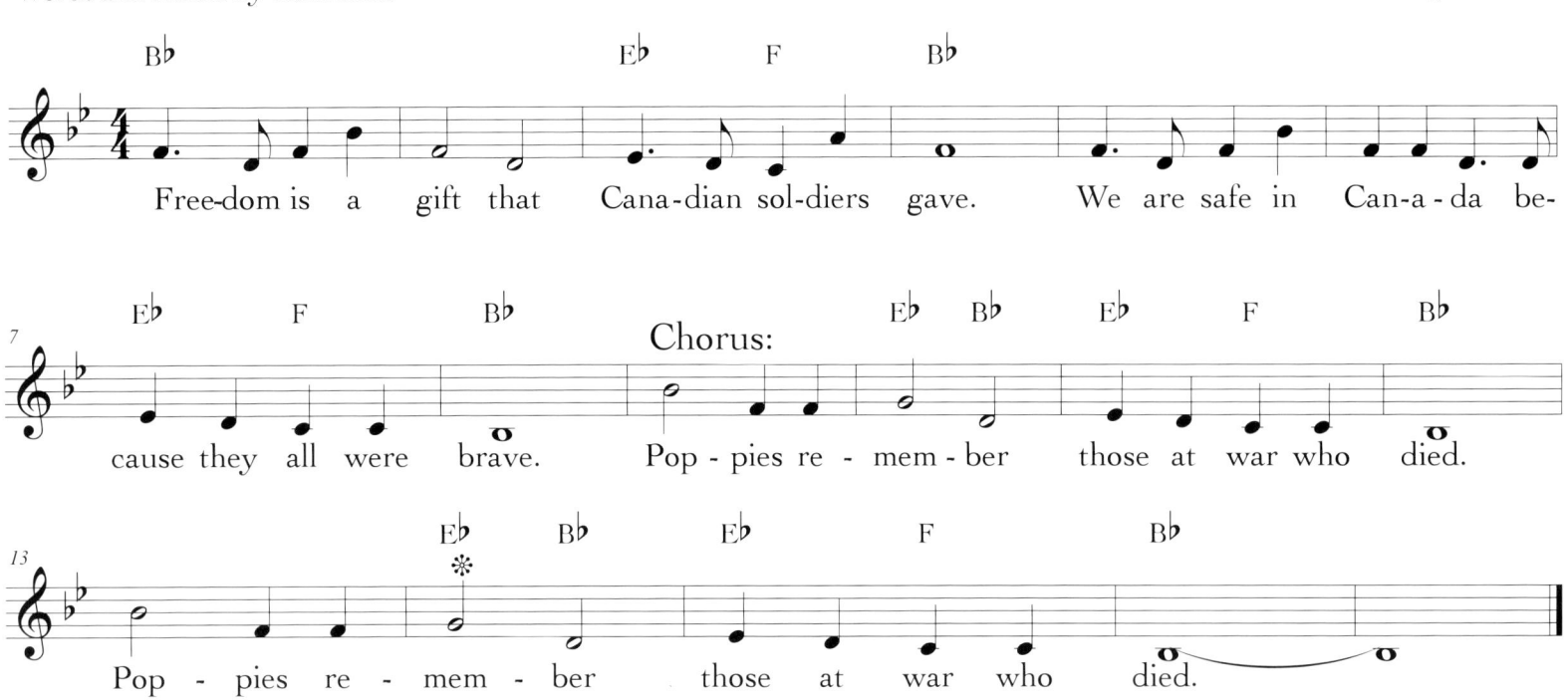

2. We're forever grateful for their courage and pride.
   Men and women gave their all, standing side by side. (chorus)

3. In the world around us, Canadians do their part.
   Keeping peace so others have a brand new start. (chorus)

4. We wear our poppies proudly, we never shall forget.
   Canadian troops are heroes, we're forever in their debt. (chorus)

Jean Miso is a proud Canadian who lives in Toronto with her husband Dan and two sons Emerson and Austin. She teaches music to children with developmental disabilities, and the song "We'll Never Forget" was initially written for a Remembrance Day service conducted at her school. Jean was educated at York and Brock Universities. She holds a BFA in music composition, a BA in psychology, a BEd and a MEd in curriculum studies.

From an early age, Jean emphasized remembrance of our Canadian Forces. In Grade 7, she entered a Royal Canadian Legion poetry contest, and her poem "11th Day of November" placed first. "We'll Never Forget" advances the sentiments she expressed at age 12, and she hopes that this book—which also conveys the diversity of Canada's culture and landscape—will inspire youth to pay tribute to the heroic deeds of our Canadian military.

www.jeanmiso.ca

Jean Miso
Author and Music Composer

"My work was a mix of fact and imagination, attempting to capture in a few images something of the breadth of the Canadian experience in general and an appreciation in particular for those who serve and have sacrificed for our country."

Asher Sadeh received his BFA in the Department of Advertising Design and Visual Communication in 1967 and his MFA (majoring in painting and art history) from Pratt Institute in New York City in 1972.

He has taught art in a high school in New York and worked as the assistant to the curator of the youth wing at the Israel Museum in Jerusalem. He has taught painting, drawing, art history and photography at Georgian College in Barrie, Ontario, and he has taught drawing at the Art Gallery of Ontario. He was an instructor in the off-campus MFA program of Norwich University's Vermont College. He has also worked as a freelance photographer, illustrator and portrait painter.

Asher has participated in over 50 group and solo painting and photography exhibitions in New York, Utah, Washington, Ontario and Israel. He is a member of the Ontario Society of Artists and resides with his family in Richmond Hill, Ontario.

www.ashersadeh.com

Asher Sadeh
Artist

15th Battalion Memorial Project Team

From left to right: Captain (Ret.) Steve Gilbert, CD; Honorary Lieutenant-Colonel John Newman; Brigadier-General (Ret.) Greg Young, OMM, CD; and Captain (Ret.) Victor Goldman, CD.